# EARTH PRINTS

## Expressions of Beauty in Experiences

Janine E. Janosky

and

Dora J. Moscatello

AugustSolutionsGroup LLC

http://augustsolutionsgroup.com

Earth Prints

Expressions of Beauty in Experience

As the wonder of the universe unfolds around humanity, each season calls our memories, our astonishment at what we see and feel around us, and the renewal of a chance for new experience. The beauty of our physical environment and of our experiences is to be savored and shared through our expressions to self and others. The natural world serves to reflect our human joy, suffering, and wonder, as we express through poetry and visual artistry. Through photography and poetry, this book seeks to capture the physical, emotional, and spiritual essences that we share through our natural world. Immerse yourself, as the poetry and visual artistry seek to share our collective journey. Whitespaces intentionally available near photographs to provide opportunities to call upon your similar and same experiences as the universe leads the way into its eternal mystery.

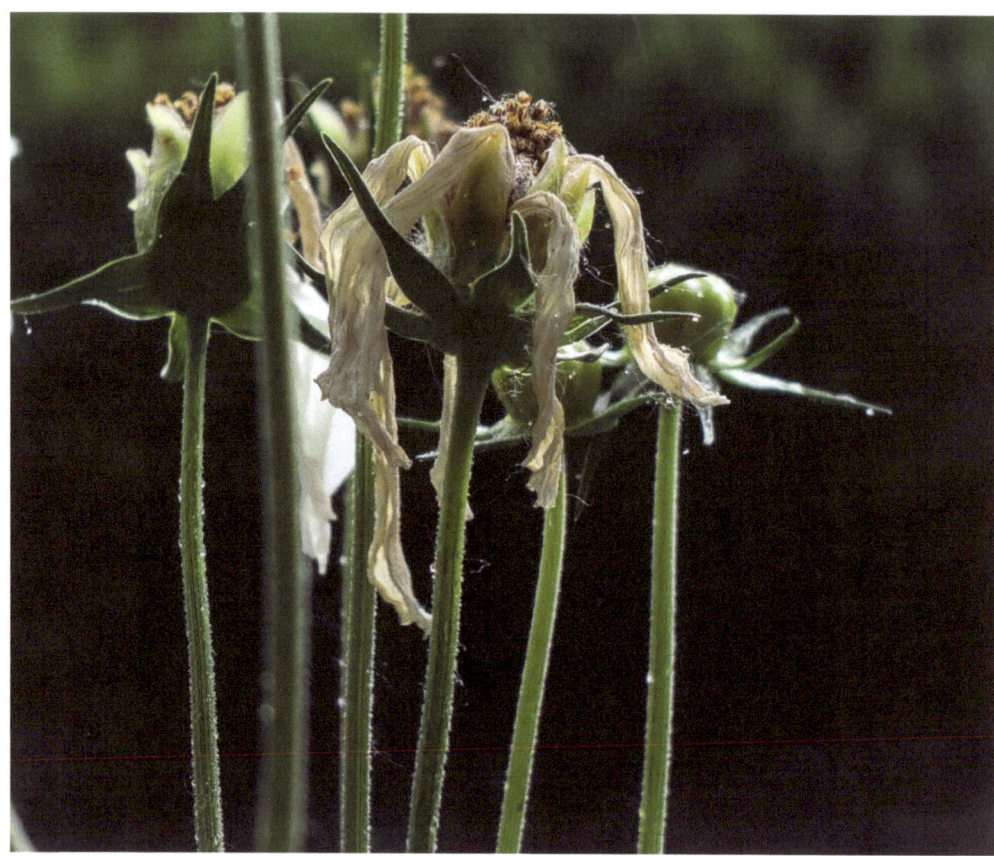

Autumn

Ever sad season.

The tree outside my window
Brushes in the wind against the house
To confirm that it still holds life in its dark belly
Although its arms look dead
It whispers with gathering boldness
To call my attention

It moves with balletic grace and shakes off
No longer necessary pink and russet scales
Mourning its recent verdure.

After the wind and the shedding and the rains
It waits still and patiently
For the winter that is coming.

Changing in a constant rhythm
Inside and out
This tree is life
This tree is me.

Snowprint

Twisted feet of birds make the same
Lace pattern in snow;

Angles of light show paper tracings
under the streetlight's fish-eye lens
A macrocosm of thread and shadows.
Children making angel wings in the snow
are destroying the mood. . .

Looking through the white plain of ice
I sense the blacktop, brick, and gum
Beneath the cool beauty and sparkle.
I'm cold.

The Cold

My breath is solid
Choking me with stubborn ice
Winter wants my death.

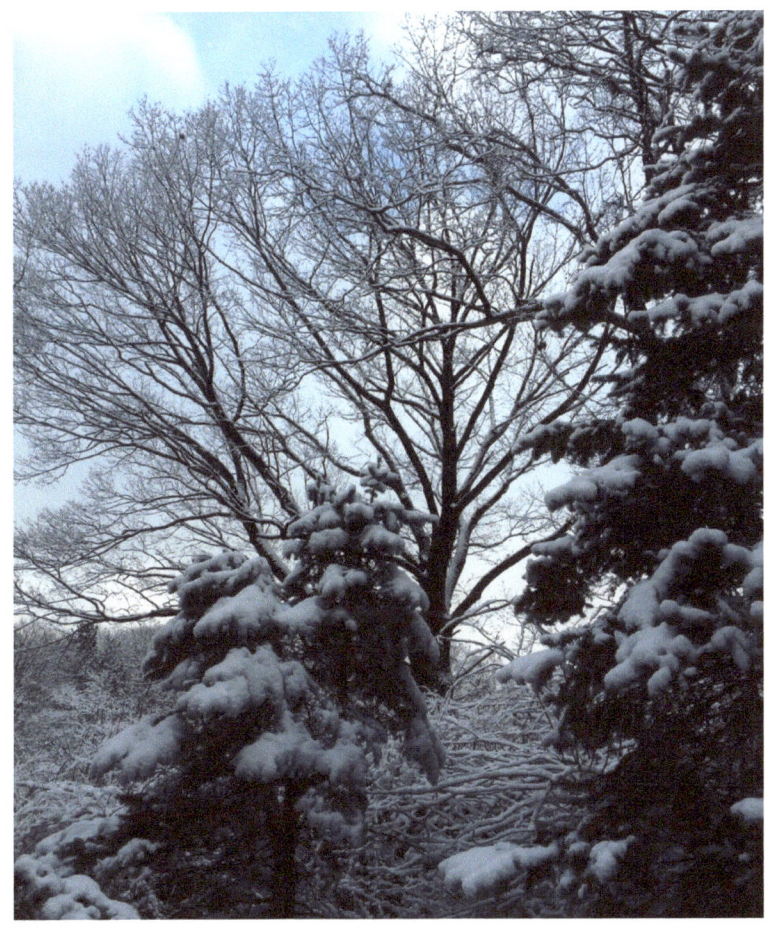

Wind Storm

Two nights ago fierce winds descended,
        screamed through the woods.
I lay in bed uneasy, fearful, dreading the morning's reveal.
Dead branches rolling across the roof,
Projectiles hurtling, windows shaking, winds protesting at the door.
Chimes clanging ever faster in a frightful cacophony.
Then silence.

Aeolus sends his siren song on wind, to beckon, summon me.
Standing in the still dark yard with no audience
I dance as a Dervish dances, as the wind resumes to move with me.
Raised arms to the heavens and palms stretched upward to catch
        the moon's rays.
It approaches a pure ecstasy, much like the fervor of new love, and
I lose all balance and fall, remembering nothing after.

I awake at sunlight in my bed as from a dream
to find matted leaves on the bottom of my gown,
        a black twig beside my feet.

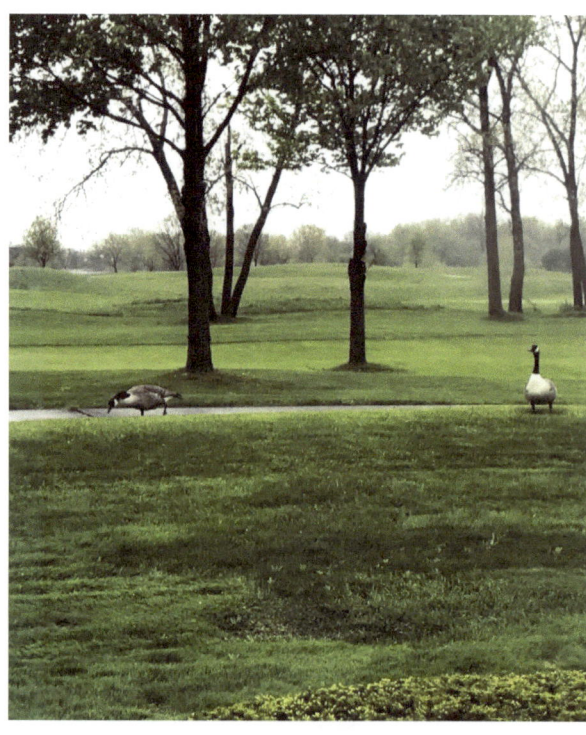

Perfect Weapon

I fear icicles. . . .
Pendant from the roof's
    edge, glistening,
Gaining strength and length
    each hour
Hardening at night into
    something deadly
Becoming the perfect weapon

Imagine one breaks loose
Plunges innocently or with
    malice into your heart
and melts away into nothingness

No weapon found at the scene.

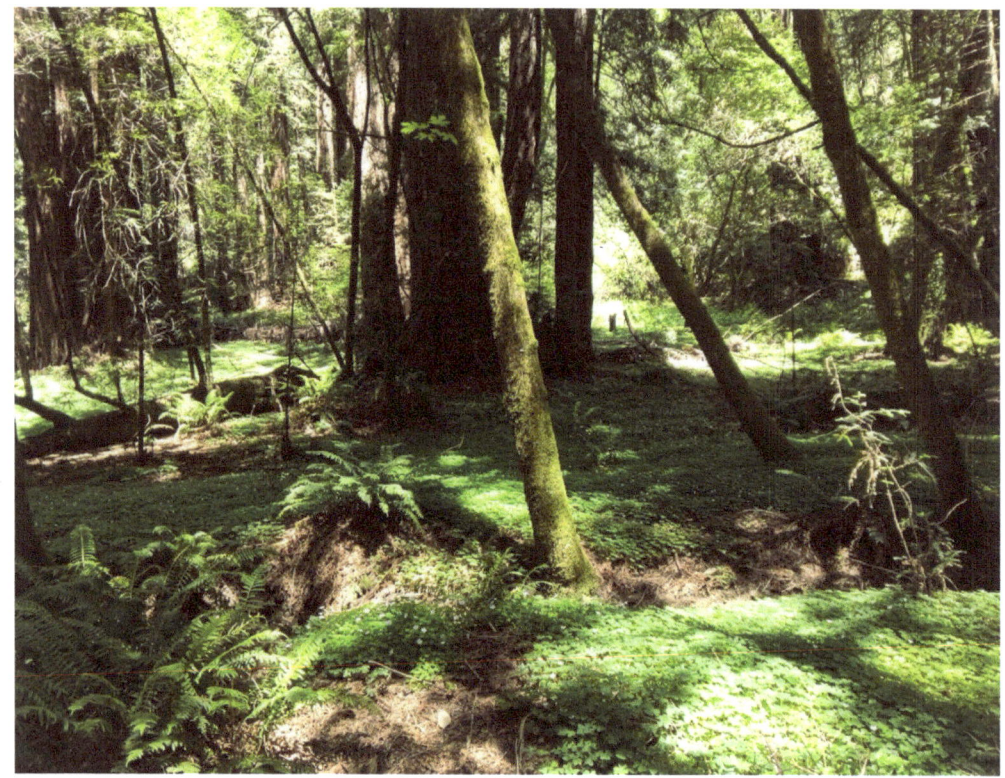

Green Peace

The bright green omnibus passes without noise through
        the sky
On its winding way to who knows where.

I rode for a time, but all the stops I
        planned on making
were already filled.

The conductor looks familiar but I can't
        recognize his face.
And all the faces I have known are
        passengers on the bus.

They get on and off, never seeming to need
        a ticket.

I am trying desperately to get off at
        the next green spot.
It's my garden of Eden.

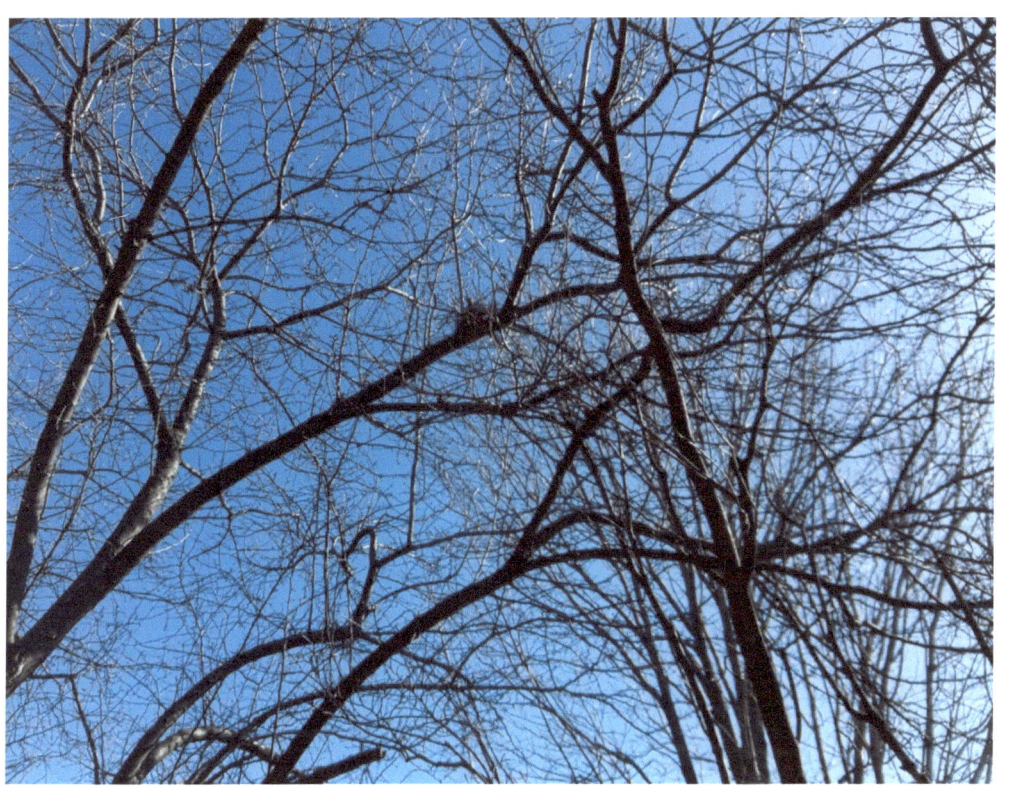

Winter is Coming

I waited for autumn colors and freefall leaves
to call me to the season.
I open the door to premature icy moisture and harsh winds,
and my anticipation is thwarted.
Wind chimes crash loudly in the distance, announcing that
Queen Winter will reign in the end.

I bemoan the dry and dying leaves succumbing
to the mire underfoot, but Winter comes too soon,
bringing solace and cleansing and pure light to
smooth the earth and life's rough edges.
Angels flutter near, annointing us with their snow gifts.

My Neighbor's Oak

My neighbor cut down his vibrant oak tree today,
Or rather he hired five men to do the deed.

It took them six hours to hack away its life,
Climbing, cursing, cutting, yelling, joking, sawing. . .
The one in the cherry picker took particular glee
in rendering its elegant arms into lifeless stubs.

Watching from my window I lament its passing,
Flashbacks of its verdant abundance providing respite from the hot suns
        of swiftly approaching warm climate.
Its jubilant palette of colors each fall in gold, sienna, Van Dyke brown, russet, and carmine.
Strong stripped black finger branches creeping over to touch even my windows
        with their rat tat tat in the wind.
Harlequin patterns of snow and bark as winter winds blow against it
        trying to shake it loose from its decades long mooring.
Cold water droplets hanging unsuccessfully onto the lovely branches.

Squirrels have played there for years, screeching as they deliver it of
        meaty acorns, racing down to earth to secret away their treasure.
How many avian friends have called it home, born families, and moved on.

This night it is gone, no trace remains save a slight mound of sawdust
        reminiscent of the trunk yanked from its place and pulverized.

I boldly asked my neighbor why.  His reply:  too many leaves.

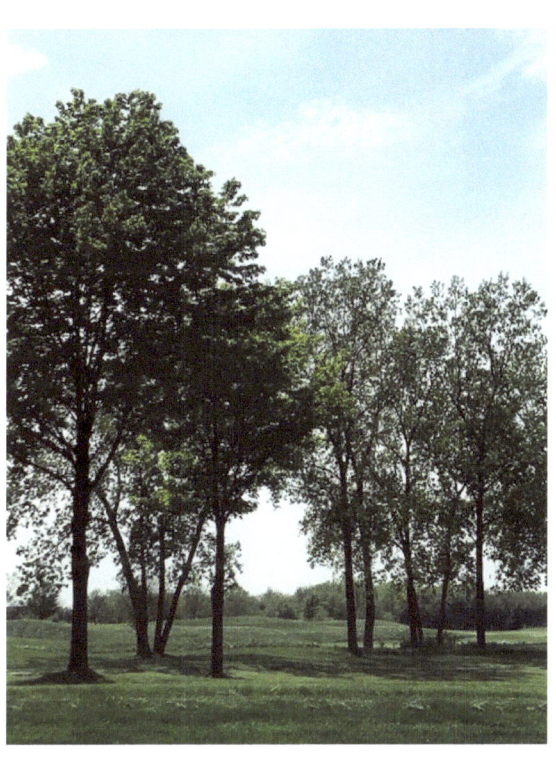

My Neighbor's Oak

Fifty years or so I have stood proud and straight
in this lackluster yard,
The only real and live entity
          among garden gnomes and wire and brick borders.

Sharing my cool shade
Harboring squirrel families
Nestling countless birds in my obscure crannies
Throwing down meaty acorns to hoard in winter's
          dearth of sustenance.
Sheltering a myriad throng of insects and living beings.
Tunneling underground with my countless roots to hold
          This lonely yard in place.
Flirting shamelessly with my kaleidoscope of golds and reds
          and browns in fall.
Braving the brunt of harsh winds as they dart toward the house in
          the dead of winter.

Roots sense the ground trembling as the ominous truck and chipper arrive.
Ropes thrown up and around my long strong arms.
Shouting, yelling, cursing, laughing all the while as men cut away my strength.
My particular hatred for the one in the cherry picker as he slices with glee
          at my lovely branches.
Hours pass and then it is done.  I am done.

What gave you the right to end my existence?  Am I not a plant
          creature put on the earth by the Universe?
          I am a spirit of long ago
          and futures to come.
               You cannot own me.
               Not ever.

Do not be disquieted.
My seed has spread to far places, and I will persist.

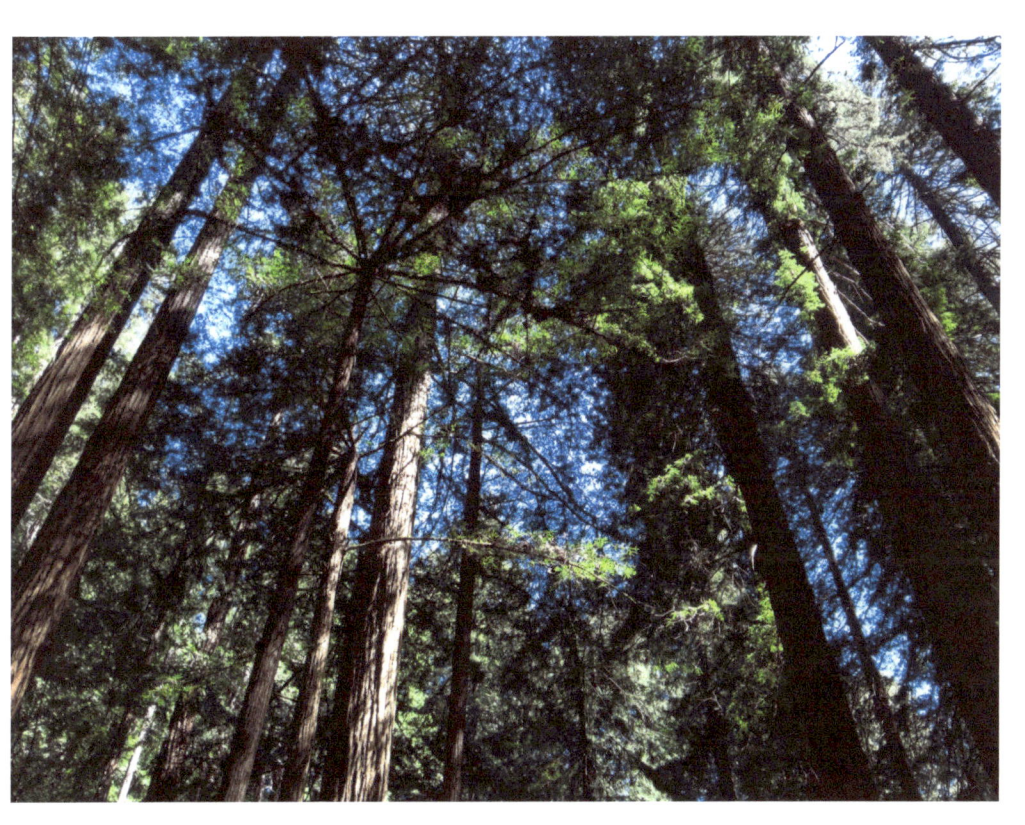

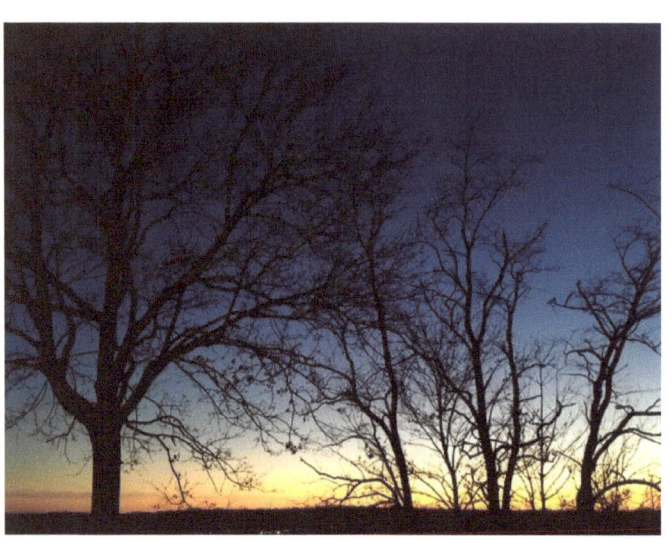

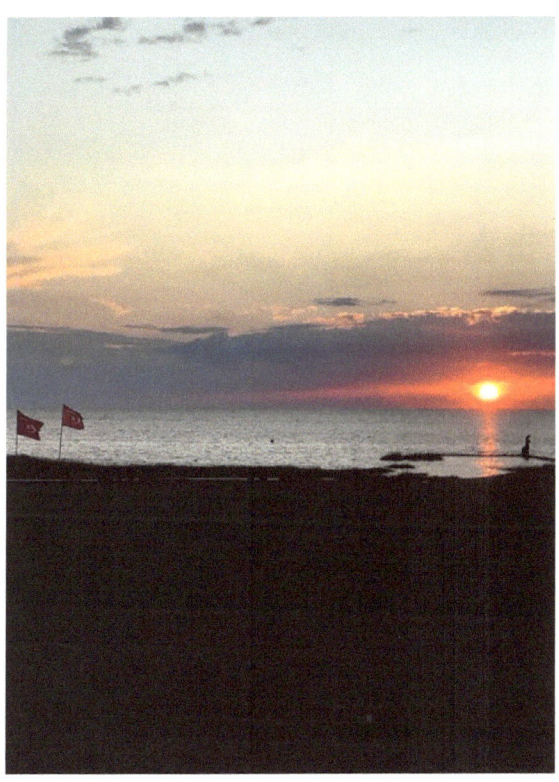

## Journey

My secrets, my griefs.
I carry them in a suitcase
As though a trip will help. . . .

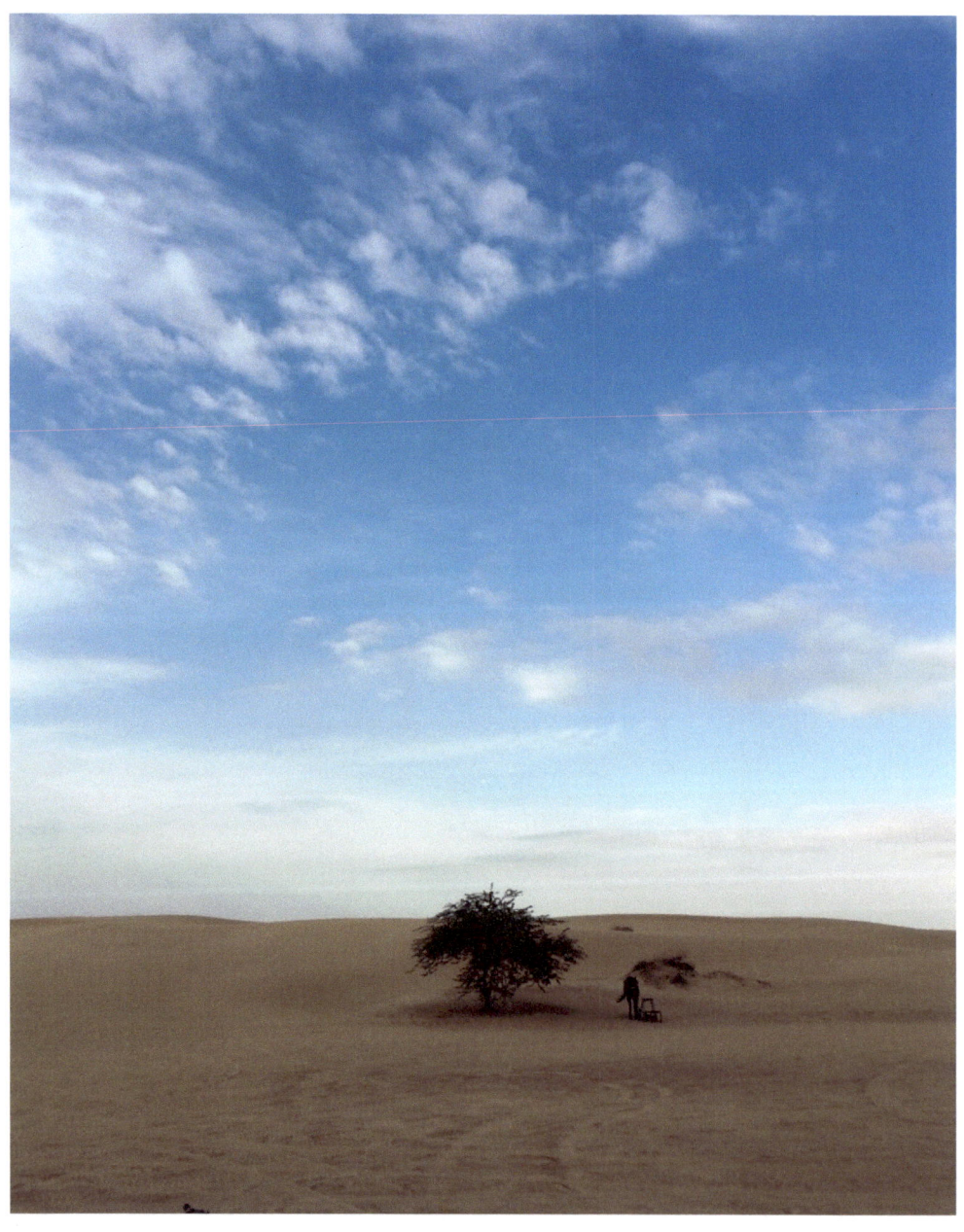

Salvo

The ocean howls its relentless roar
     this morning just after dawn.

Wind too fierce for many brings
     one single gull.
Gliding more than flying, he is either
     lost or bringing a message like
     ravens of old.

Old men with their dogs come out
     early on such mornings.
The wind helping them along on their way.
As they retrace their steps on the sand. . . .

Morning of the second day.

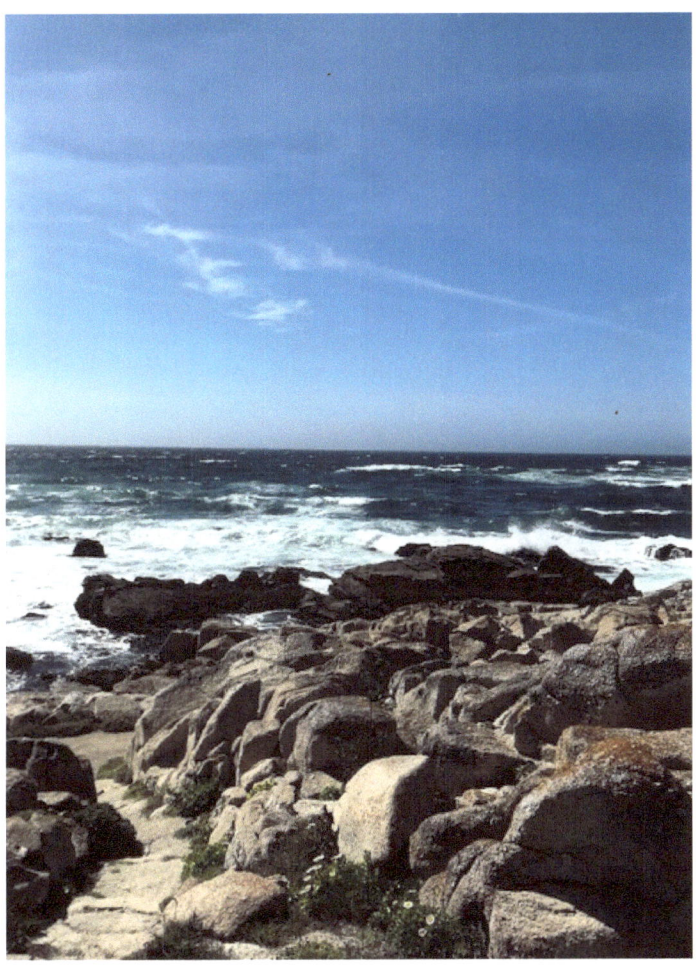

Crow's Nest

Here on this lonely perch between
        the ether and the sand,
I feel a part of both and of neither.

A space between tranquility and the rush of cortisol.
The middle ground that I have been
        seeking.
And now it lifts me up.

My salvation.

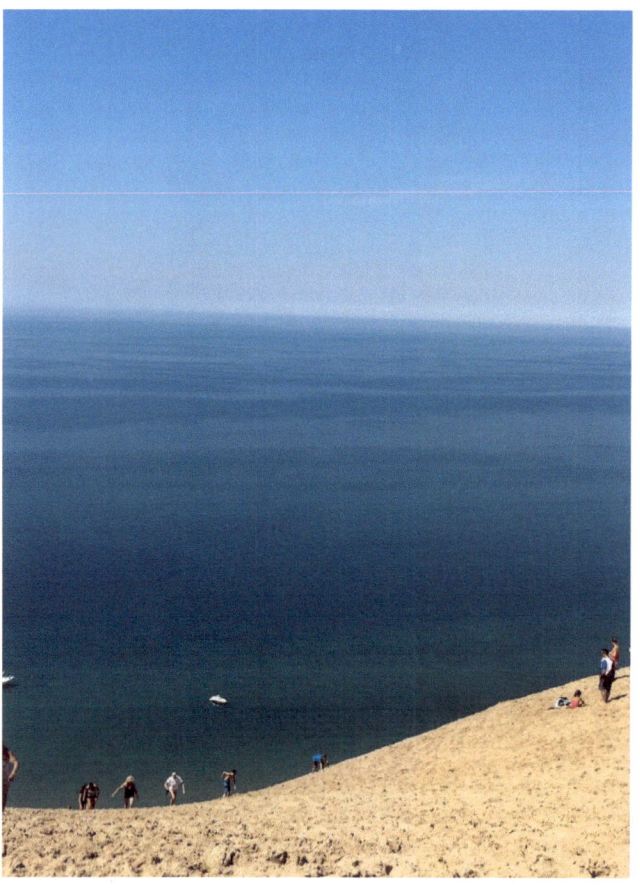

Thalassa

Sea grass and pines and low scrub.
Wind parting my hair like some
    slick comb.

Clouds hanging low to serve as
overlords of the sea,
Whitecaps rising higher and higher
beckon me to
        the eternal watery mother.

Finally time to do everything
    and nothing. . . .
What draws me here again and
 yet again?

There is no life and death here,
Only being.

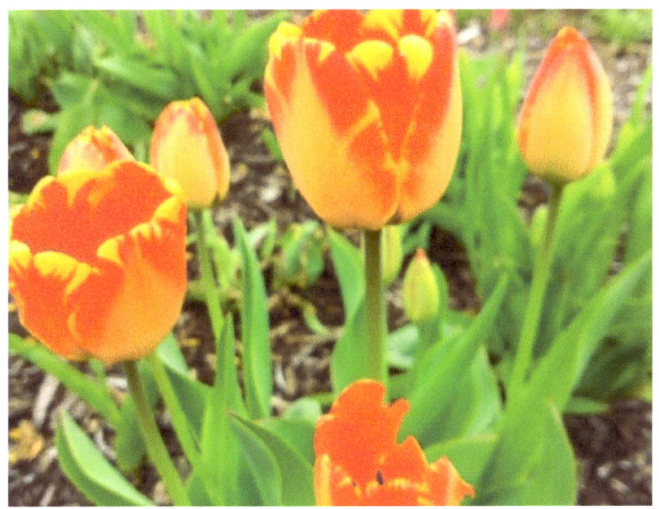

Birthing

The fecund earth has labored for nine or so months
To harbor her myriad offspring until their collective births.

And now, albeit with harsh cold and biting wind, they begin
To emerge from their earthy cocoons
In hues of purple only meant heretofore for royalty,
With yellowness that pales the sun
And blues that rival clear sharp blue eyes.

Witnessed each new spring, the birth still comes with awe
Although long awaited, still comes unexpectedly
Like searching through the crowd at the station
For the familiar face of the loved one stepping off the train.

Expected, hoped for, anticipated, and yet astounding when it
arrives.

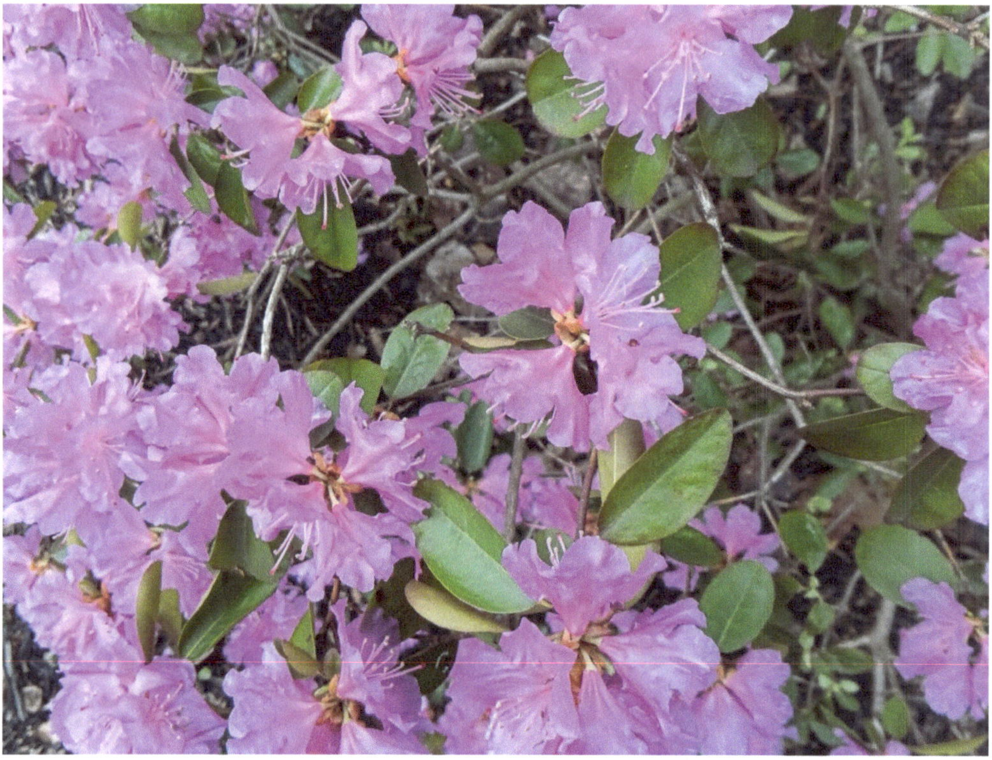

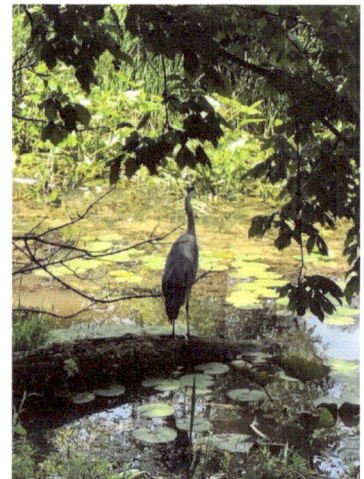

Return of Hope

The vibrant sun makes lacy patterns on the snow blanket,
Fooling us with its bright beauty.
Too frigid are the days and too icy the nights
Yet to allow any green specimen to show its timid self.

Knowing the frail violets and grape hyacinths lie in wait
For the sun's warmth to call them forward from their cold enclaves
Gives me hope and joy and anticipation
For the affirming renewal to come.

This morning life springs up once more as a tiny yellow crocus
      beneath my mighty oak tree.

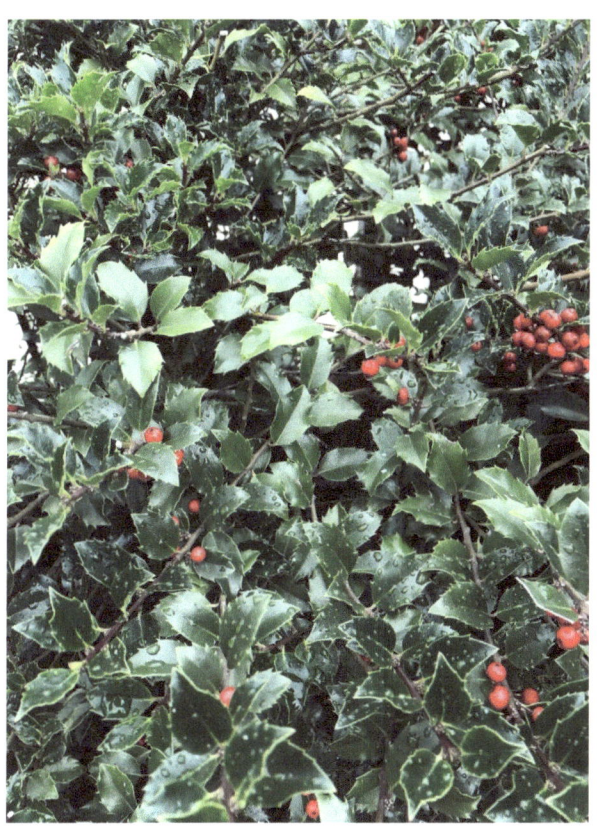

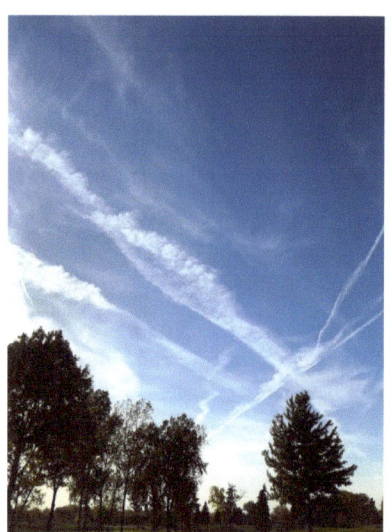

Night Train

In between wake and slumber
I slide toward vertigo as the black bullet Amtrak
cleaves the clinging darkness.

Tiny windows of dim light in faraway houses
struggle to illumine the way
Through the inky half way of the night.

What inchoate action starts up behind these diminutive flickers?
Who is crying?
Who fighting?
Who being loved?
What child being soothed?
What worries and shames timidly shared?
What whispers barely heard under the covers?
Who reveling in the sweet touch of a loved one?
Who retching through another night of sickness?
What unspeakable secrets being shared in the dark?
Who reaching for the dog's soft head during desperate dreams?
Who screaming the birthing cry that brilliantly slices the quiet?
Who passing into the personal Elysium of nothingness and death?

Possibilities hold hostage any thought of sleep.
I dream of being behind each window
The dream fills me up at once with terror and longing.
The train persists. . . .

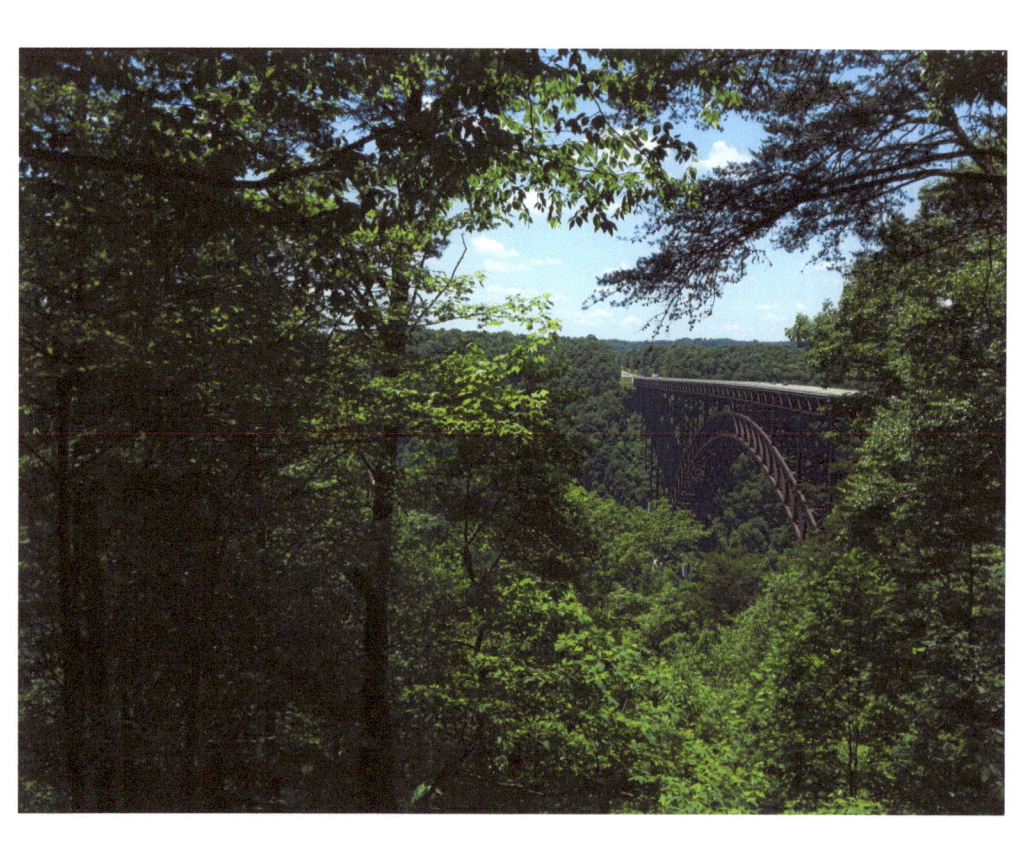

Janine E. Janosky has a life-long drive to positively improve the quality of life for all, with her work spanning more than three decades.  As we work to improve our world, this provides for an exploration, consideration, and appreciation of impactful innovative paradigms.  Her prolific written and visual work has appeared in multiple venues from biomedical journals to popular publications.

Dora J. Moscatello has spent her professional career serving in the scientific publishing industry.  Her expressive passion has been as a life-long poet and artist, expressing the beauty of life through her work and concentrating on the natural world and the possibilities of the human condition.

www.ingramcontent.com/pod-product-compliance
Lightning Source LLC
Chambersburg PA
CBHW041121180526
45172CB00001B/366